HOPE for the Family:

The Power of Prayer and Fasting

Lisa C. Turner
Author

Unless otherwise indicated, Scripture references are taken
from Kings James version of the Holy Bible copyright 1982
Thompson Chain, Inc.

CONTENTS

DEDICATION

I dedicate this book to my Lord and Savior Jesus Christ for choosing to use me as a message of HOPE and for His continued faithfulness that proves, there is Power in Prayer!

To my husband, Deacon Lawrence Turner, Jr., a humble servant and man after God's own heart! Thank you for your love and leadership! I am honored to be your wife! You can count on me to fight for our family on the right battlefield. (Ephes. 6:12)

Eyes have not seen and neither have ears heard the things God has prepared for you...

~ I love you!

INTRODUCTION

Fasting is a biblical principle that draws us closer to God through self-denial. Fasting should always have a purpose and be accompanied with prayer otherwise, it is merely a restricted diet. The word of God declares that we can decree a thing and the Lord our God will establish it for us!

Our focus for these Fasts is to let the enemy know that we have the Victory!

Unless otherwise noted, the instructions for all Fasts are as follows:

Time: 6 a.m. - 6 p.m.
What: Water and Juice

After 6 p.m. - One meal consisting of any of the following: baked or broiled chicken/fish, steamed veggies, salad, water, juice, or tea.

Note: Let's make this a time to shut out ALL distractions (extensive chatting, etc.) and really allow the Lord to strengthen us as we hunger and thirst for more of him.

**Please consult with your physician before participating in these Fasts.

Stay encouraged and HOPE in God!

"If you want to see change in any situation, you must first see yourself in the situation."

~Archbishop Alfred A. Owens, Jr.

Confess your faults one to another, and pray one for another, that ye may be healed. The effectual fervent prayer of a righteous man availeth much.
(James 5:16)

SOUND THE ALARM

Praise the Lord Women of God,

This is the day the Lord has made, let us rejoice and be glad in it.

The Lord led me to begin this 3-Day Fast by first introducing my position to you. I believe it is not until we allow the Holy Spirit to help us become transparent that others can feel free to open up and thereby be transformed by the renewing of their mind. My sisters, though our situations may differ, you are not alone. I borrow the words of Paul to give you the foundation of my faith and focus as follows:

"I'm not saying that I have this all together, that I have it made. But I am well on my way, reaching out for Christ, who has so wondrously reached out for me. Friends, don't get me wrong: By no means do I count myself an expert in all of this, but I've got my eye on the goal, where God is beckoning us onward to Jesus. I'm off and running and I'm not turning back. So let's keep focused on that goal, those of us who want everything God has for us. If any of you have something else in mind, something less than total commitment, God will clear your blurred vision you'll see it yet! Now that we're on the right track, let's stay on it!" (Philippians 3:13-15) (MSG)

DAY ONE: REFOCUS

"I will lift up mine eyes to the hills from whence cometh my help. My help cometh from the Lord, which made heaven and earth". (Psalm 121:1-2) (KJV)

Let us pray,

Good Morning Holy Spirit,

We love you! You are welcome into our hearts and minds. We declare that there is nobody like you! We thank you for another day of your grace and mercy. We ask you to forgive us of all unrighteousness, negative attitudes and words, behaviors, unwise decisions, doubt, fear, and anything that is not pleasing to you. We come to you open and honest with sincere hearts saying it's me, it's me, it's me oh Lord, standing in the need of prayer! We need you to refocus our minds and renew our strength so that we can recover all you have promised us. Most of all, we want to stand strong as women of God, pleasing in your sight. We thank you for being so faithful! You have been a very present help in the time of trouble. Because you're in control, we know you have not allowed any more on us than we have been able to bare. We ask that you touch our minds and give us peace that will surpass our own understanding. We want our hearts to be filled with your joy. We know that in the presence of the Lord there is fullness of joy and at your right hand there are pleasures forever more!

We thank you for being our God! We know that all things are working together for our good because we love you! We place every situation into your hands because you do all things well. We believe that as we do so, you will keep us from falling into the plot and plans of the enemy. We surrender our will to you. We walk not after the works of the flesh but in the fruit of your Holy Spirit. Thank you for changing our thoughts and aligning them with your word. We are more than conquerors in the name of Jesus name, Amen.

REFOCUS

Refocus: to bring into focus or alignment; to converge or cause to converge; of ideas or emotions.

"Summing it all up, friends, I'd say you'll do best by filling your minds and meditating on things true, noble, reputable, authentic, compelling, gracious—the best, not the worst; the beautiful, not the ugly; things to praise, not things to curse. Put into practice what you learned from me, what you heard and saw and realized. Do that, and God, who makes everything work together, will work you into his most excellent harmonies". (Philippians 4:8-9) (MSG)

Food for thought:

Can God trust you to stand and refuse to bow to the distractions and unpleasant issues in your life? So you say, "Enlarge my territory, increase me" What if God is increasing your faith to trust him to sustain you in this situation? Refocus and know that through your obedience, God can change the heart of someone else which will change your situation. Yes, that someone or situation that looks like, talks like, acts like they're not or it's not going to change. Read the book of Daniel. When he found himself in a situation where he had to choose to obey the will of God or bow to the king, he obeyed God. God used Daniel to prove that he honors faithfulness and then gave him favor with the King. As in this story, the heart of your (you fill in the blank) is in the hands of God. Remain faithful, do it God's way because He IS in control!

"Now faith is the substance of things hoped for, the evidence of things not seen".
(Hebrews 11:1) (MSG)

Women of God, if we're going to believe God for anything, we must believe Him for EVERYTHING!

Stay encouraged and HOPE in God!

DAY TWO: RENEWED STRENGTH

"And he said unto me, my grace is sufficient for thee: for my strength is made perfect in weakness".
(2 Corinthians 12:9a) (KJV)

Let us pray,

Dear Heavenly Father,

Great is thy faithfulness unto to us. We come before your presence with thanksgiving in our hearts. We thank you for another opportunity to praise you for who you are. You are an Awesome God! You're in a class all by yourself. You are Wonder of Wonders, King of Kings and Lord of Lords. If we had ten thousand tongues we could not praise you enough. There is nobody like you!

Father, we come boldly before your throne of grace asking that you wash and cleanse us from all unrighteousness in the name of Jesus. We love you and more than anything we want to be pleasing to you in all that we do. We come before you as virtuous women asking you to strengthen us with your grace to endure the issues in our lives. Give us patience to run the race that you have set before us. We come to you because you are our present help, and our everlasting strength. We know there is no thing too hard for you. We surrender our will to you so that you may fill us with wisdom and direction. You said if we trust in you with all of our heart and lean not to our own understanding you would direct our path. We need you to show us what to do. We stand still in your presence waiting on you. You promised to hear and answer our prayers so we won't move to the left or to the right without hearing from you. We surrender everything and everyone to you. We believe you will perfect that which concerns us. We pray for strength to trust you even when we cannot trace you. We know you are with us because you promised never to leave nor forsake us. Thank you for your keeping power! There is no way we would have made it this far without you. We praise you for renewing our minds with strength to endure the process to every promised blessing. We die to the will of our flesh and press on toward the mark for the prize of the high calling in Christ Jesus, Amen!

RENEWED STRENGTH

RENEWED STRENGTH: to restore or replenish

But they that wait upon the LORD shall renew their strength; they shall mount up with wings as eagles; they shall run, and not be weary; and they shall walk, and not faint. (Isaiah 40:31) (KJV)

Food for thought:
There are times in life when issues can weigh on us so heavy, and yes, practically zap every ounce of your strength. The good news about God is that his strength is made perfect in our weakness. I encourage you to step back and rest in the finished

11

work of Jesus Christ. He's already overcome the struggles of this world therefore, He is able to keep you from falling! His word declares we can look to the hills from whence cometh our help because our help comes from the Lord! He gives power when we are weak and increases our strength just when we need him most!

From the end of the earth will I cry unto thee, when my heart is overwhelmed: lead me to the rock that is higher than I. For thou hast been a shelter for me, and a strong tower from the enemy; I will abide in thy tabernacle forever: I will trust in the covert of thy wings. Selah. (Psalm 61:2-4) (KJV)

Women of God, endure your hardships as a good soldier and know that, God's got your back!

Stay encouraged and HOPE in God!

DAY THREE: RECOVER

"Rejoice in the Lord always and again I say rejoice". (Philippians 4:4)

Let us pray,

Father in the name of Jesus, we praise you for another day of life, health and strength. We thank you for including us in your plan for such a time as this. We ask for your forgiveness of all sins and pray that you will continue to make and mold us into the women of God you are calling us to be. Thank you for helping us through these past 3 days of prayer and fasting. We know our strength comes from you alone. We pray that you will continue to strengthen us and cause what you have spoken to rest in our hearts as a message of HOPE. Now God, I touch and agree with the prayers of every women praying and fasting these past 3 days. Father you know every issue and concern in detail. Thank you for having the power to meet each of us right where we are. Thank you for their obedience in responding to the call. Because you have chosen them for this time, I believe you have an expected end for them in mind. I pray that you will keep their minds in perfect peace and remind them to stay focused on who you are and not what their situation would dictate to them. Give them a double dose of your grace so they will be renewed daily with strength to go beyond surviving but to thrive in every area of their lives. I pray that they will seek you in all of your righteousness and know that all other things will be added unto them. Thank you for giving us the power to recover everything the enemy has taken. We praise you in advance for taking us to another level in our walk with you, for filling our thirsty souls with your righteousness, for healthy wholesome marriages, godly living in our singleness, respectful and obedient children, restored health and finances, new employment opportunities and all those things we believe you to do. Father we thirst for more of you and ask that you continue to fill us with your love and power to live a life that is pleasing in your sight. In Jesus name, Amen!

RECOVER

RECOVER- to find, get back or regain.

"They shall still bring forth fruit in old age; they shall be fat and flourishing; to show that the LORD is upright: he is my rock, and there is no unrighteousness in him". (Psalm 92:14-15)

Food for thought:

Old age: Maybe you're not old in age but what you're going through is old. You've been dealing with it for a long time. So long you wonder if God is really going to fix, change, rearrange and perfect it. The issue is so old that you've said at one time or another, "that's just the way it is, etc."

Remember, "Death and life are in the power of the tongue: and they that love it shall eat the fruit thereof". (Proverbs 18:21). In other words, you shall have what you say so, if you're going to fast, pray and believe God than speak what you expect! Yes we all go through, but do that, go through and come out with the mindset that you have the victory because God is STILL going to do it!

You shall be fat and flourishing: God is going to enlarge your territory! What's to come is better than what's been. "But as it is written, Eye hath not seen, nor ear heard, neither have entered into the heart of man, the things which God hath prepared for them that love him." (1 Corinth. 2:9). You shall receive an abundance of overflow in every area where the enemy is trying to discourage you. Just because it hasn't happened for you yet doesn't mean that God can't do it. "Wait on the LORD: be of good courage, and he shall strengthen thine heart: wait, I say, on the LORD." (Psalm 27:14) Keep your eyes on the promise. If God said it then it shall come to pass! You SHALL Recover ALL!!!

He is my rock: God is your strength! "With men this is impossible, but with God all things are possible." (Matthew 19:26). You've tried everything you know to do to fix it, change it and work it out. Now you can turn it over to the Lord and watch him work it out. There is nothing too hard for him. Delight thyself also in the LORD: and he shall give thee the desires of thine heart."

15

(Psalm 37:4). Give it to God; He can handle it and He IS STILL going to do it!!!!

Women of God, You are blessed because you believed that the Lord would do what he said. (Luke 1:45)

Stay encouraged and HOPE in God!

"If you're going to win this battle, you must be willing to fight even when it "seems" as if you're the only one fighting!"

~ Lisa C. Turner

"For we wrestle not against flesh and blood, but against principalities, against powers, against the rulers of the darkness of this world, against spiritual wickedness in high places." Ephesians 6:12

3- DAY FAST FOR THE FAMILY

Praise the Lord Women of God,

I can remember getting into several fights as a young girl and always having my sister there for back up. During one particular fight she was not only back up, but she actually pushed me into the fight because she had the confidence that we would win. Woman of God now is the time when we have to roll up our sleeves and fight for our family. The enemy is seeking to destroy the people of God by any means necessary but he's a liar from the pit of hell! I don't know if you're fighting for your marriage, children, finances, health, employment or all of the above and more. What I do know is that many are the afflictions of the righteous but the Lord delivers him from them ALL! I know that the Lord is a man of War: the Lord is His name and He's got our back!

Join us for this 3-Day fast. The biblical meaning of the number is "completion". We're coming together on one accord to let the devil know it is over! He is a liar and a defeated foe! The Holy Ghost gave me a push through my spiritual sister who reminded me that one can chase a thousand and two can put ten thousand to flight! She told me she has my back so I don't have to fight alone. Touch and Agree is saying the same to you, we've got your back, so you're not fighting alone! You can win if you don't quit because you already have the Victory!

Nay in ALL these things we are MORE than conquerors through Him that loved us!

When does the fast start? NOW! When my sister pushed me, the fight was on immediately! As soon as you read this chapter and feel a push from the Holy Ghost you need to get in the fight! Fast for at least 3 days. What is the fast menu? SACRIFICE! Whatever you are led to sacrifice that matches the blessing/deliverance you anticipate receiving from God.

Remember fasting without the word of God and prayer = diet.

Engage your weapons and know that we are fighting with and for you!

Stay encouraged and HOPE in God!

"Who can find a virtuous woman? for her price is far above rubies. The heart of her husband doth safely trust in her, so that he shall have no need of spoil. She will do him good and not evil all the days of her life."

Proverbs 31:10-13

40-DAY PRAYER AND FASTING FOR YOUR HUSBAND

Dear Virtuous Wives,

I believe the most important role of a godly wife is to pray for her husband. Our God does all things well! I count it no accident that He would call us together for prayer. I believe that as we fast and pray God is going to bring some things to an end as well as birth some new beginnings in the lives of our husbands. The bible says, whatsoever things we desire when we pray if we believe that we receive them, we shall have them. I am excited and pray that you too, and are expecting God to move!

Week 1	Salvation/Spiritual Growth
Week 2	Leadership/Marriage & Family
Week 3	Commitment
Week 4	Communication
Week 5	Health/Prosperity
Week 6	Relationships

I encourage you to read Ephesians 6:10-18 prior to beginning this 40-Day period of Prayer and Fasting.

Stay encouraged and HOPE in God!

WEEK ONE: SALVATION/SPIRITUAL GROWTH

Let us pray,

Oh Lord our God how Excellent is your name in all the earth! Father we come in a spirit of unity touching and agreeing with your Holy Spirit on behalf of our spouses. Before we ask anything of you, we first want to repent of all unrighteousness and pray you will forgive us in the name of Jesus. We come before you repenting for anytime we have been out of order concerning our roles as godly wives. We ask you to strengthen us so that praying for our husbands will continue to be a priority and not something we do just in times of trouble. We pray even now that you will honor our time of fasting and prayer as we stand in the gap on their behalf.

Now God we lift every spouse represented. We thank you for your word that says you are not slack concerning your promises towards them. We ask that you save the unsaved, remove the stony heart and give them a heart of flesh so may come to know you in the pardon of their sins. Create in them a clean heart and renew within them a right spirit in Jesus name. Father we pray for those who know you but have turned away from your will. We thank you for the good work you have begun, and know you are able to finish what you started in their lives. We ask that you give them a heart of repentance and restore them back into a right relationship with you. Strengthen those who have taken up their cross to follow hard after you. We pray that you keep them encouraged so they do not become weary in well doing. Increase their desire to know you more intimately and let them know that you have greater work for them to do. We pray for a double anointing to rest upon our husbands that will cause demons to tremble and flee as they declare your name, Jesus! We pray that you give them a hunger and thirst for your righteousness like never before. Develop a strong bond with them to trust in you alone and lean not to their own understanding. Strengthen them spiritually and cause them to trust you even when they cannot trace you. We ask that you stir up the gift within them and remind them that they can do all things through you. We cancel the plans of the enemy over our husbands. We declare that no weapon formed against them will prosper. We come against principalities, powers, rulers of the darkness of this world, and spiritual wickedness in high places. We bind the spirit of fear, and loose love, power and a sound mind. We loose holy boldness that will give them courage to walk in the purpose you have created for their lives. We invite your Holy Spirit to rule and reign as you lead and guide them into all truth.

We plead the blood of Jesus against anything that will hinder their spiritual growth and relationship with you. We give you praise for these mighty men of valour. We thank you for their salvation and for strengthening them so that your purpose will be fulfilled in their lives. To God be all the Glory in Jesus name, Amen!

Declaration: I declare by faith that (your husband's name) is saved, sanctified and filled with the Holy Ghost. He is a man after God's own heart. He presents himself as a living sacrifice holy and acceptable unto God. He delights himself in godly principles and will not forget the word of God. I declare that eye hath not seen, nor ear heard, neither have entered into the heart of man, the things which God hath prepared for (your husband's name) because he loves God. I declare that he IS the righteousness of God and the anointing of God is upon his life. So it is said, so shall it be, in Jesus name!

Your role: "Pray without ceasing".
(1 Thessalonians 5:17) (KJV)

Stay encouraged and HOPE in God!

WEEK TWO: LEADERSHIP/MARRIAGE & FAMILY

Let us pray,

This is the day the Lord has made, let us rejoice and be glad in it. Father in the name of Jesus we come to say thank you for another week of prayer and fasting. Once again we come in a spirit of unity touching and agreeing with your Holy Spirit on behalf of our spouses. As we begin this week, we pray for clean hands and pure hearts so that nothing will hinder our prayers from reaching you. Search our hearts Lord and if you find anything that should not be, take it out and cleanse us from all unrighteousness in Jesus name.

Father we lift our spouses to you in their role as the leader of our marriage and family. We thank you for the order you have created for the ministry of marriage. You said in your word that the husband is the head of the wife as Christ is head of the Church. We pray your continued blessings upon our husbands. We thank you for helping them be all you intended them to be. As they take their rightful place, we ask you to help us step back, love, honor, respect, and submit ourselves to their leadership in the name of Jesus. We want to honor you in all that we do. We realize that when we are out of order with our husbands, we are out of order with you! Keep us mindful that in order for our marriage to work in the way you intended we must be obedient to your commands. We come asking you to strengthen and encourage them to be godly leaders. We thank you for the greatest example of leadership we have in the life of your son Christ Jesus. We pray that our husbands will imitate the character of Christ as they assume their position. We ask your blessings upon our marriage and pray that they will be our lover and leader. Help them to lead with a heart of love and compassion. We pray that they will not abuse their role or seek to dominate the marriage through dictatorship or other negative ways. Father, when problems arise we pray that they will follow the example of Jesus and the way he was involved in working out issues and problems. We ask that you give our husbands that same mindset and the strength to face every challenge. We pray that they will seek you in all things and when they don't know what to do they will pray for wisdom in Jesus name. You said that a house divided against itself shall not stand so we bind everything that will cause division between us. We speak love and unity to our marriage so that we may please you as we operate as a team.

We speak blessings upon their fatherhood. We pray that you will teach our husbands how to be a godly example to our children. Father, we pray that our husbands will train our children in the way they should go. We know that you are able to use them to influence the lives of all of our children young and old. We ask that you give our husbands the skill to balance love, forgiveness, discipline and direction. Show them when to be a parent and when our children need them to be a friend. Build their relationship in such a way that our children will respect them as the head of the home and feel comfortable coming to them about anything. We pray that their example will teach our daughters what to expect in a mate and teach our sons how to treat and respect women in Jesus name. We ask that you heal those areas that have been broken by issues of the past. Give our husbands a heart of forgiveness and the desire to have relationship with all of their children. We bind the works of the enemy over our husbands and their role as leader. We plead the blood of Jesus over their hearts and minds. We cast down every imagination and high thing that would exalt itself against the knowledge and will of God. We break down every barrier that will hinder our husbands in anyway. Father, we thank you for Godly leadership. We pray that you continue to reassure them that they can do all things through you and that you are with them always, in Jesus name, Amen!

Declaration: I declare by faith that (your husband's name) is the Godly Priest of our home. He takes his leadership and spiritual responsibilities seriously. (your husband's name) is a good father and does not provoke his children to wrath but brings them up in the training and admonition of the Lord. He builds our home with wisdom and he is led by the spirit of God and not by the work of his flesh. He walks in integrity and his children are blessed after him.

Your role: "Pray without ceasing".
(1 Thessalonians 5:17) (KJV)
"As the church submits to Christ, so you wives should submit to your husbands in everything".
(Ephesians 5:24) (NLT)

"In the same way, you wives must accept the authority of your husbands. Then, even if some refuse to obey the Good News, your godly lives will speak to them without any words. They will be won over". (1 Peter 3:1) (NLT)

Stay encouraged and HOPE in God!

WEEK THREE: COMMITMENT

Let us pray,

I will lift up mine eyes unto the hills from whence cometh my help. My help cometh from the Lord which made heaven and earth. Father in the name of Jesus we come seeking your help on behalf of our spouses. We come drawing near to you with all our heart in the assurance that you are faithful to do all that you have promised. Before we petition you on their behalf, we ask you to forgive us from anything we have said, done or thought that did not please you. Cleanse us with hyssop, and we shall be clean, wash us and we shall be whiter than snow, in the name of Jesus.

We lift our spouses to you in the area of commitment to the marriage. We praise you for ordaining marriage as Holy matrimony. Your word says if we love you then we will keep your commandments. Father we come with the understanding that commitment works both ways because you said the two shall become one flesh. In order for us to blend together as one, we both must remain committed to the vows we spoke before you. Therefore, as we pray for our husbands, we ask you to keep us mindful that you are holding us accountable for our commitment as well. Teach us how to be virtuous wives like the woman in Proverbs 31. Show us ourselves and then help us to be better in every area of our role as a godly wife.

We come asking you to help our husbands remain faithful and committed to our marriage. Teach them how to love and respect us as you have commanded in your word. As we go through different seasons in our marriage, show them how to be sensitive to the issues we have as women. Give them a mind to do whatever it takes in making our marriage work a priority. We pray that you strengthen them in every area of weakness and give them hope to endure all things. Remind them that there is no temptation that you have not already conquered. When the enemy rushes in like a flood, we pray that you will lift up a standard that will destroy his plans in the name of Jesus. Your word says love covers a multitude of sin. Help us to be quick to forgive and not angry, discouraged, or hold unforgiveness in our hearts. Give us the same kind of love for each other that you have in forgiving us when we disappoint you. Father we pray blessings upon the intimacy in our marriage. Let us not withhold our bodies from one another. You said the marriage bed is undefiled. We pray that you cover our intimacy and show us new creative ways to please one another in Jesus name. We pray that you strengthen the bond of love, commitment, and friendship between us. Help us appreciate one another and spend time together by doing the simple things like taking walks together, saying "I love you" more often, and all those things that keep marriages refreshed in the name of Jesus.

We plead the blood of Jesus over their minds and cancel every trick and trap that has been sent to get them off course and cause division in our marriage. We loose your word that says, what you have joined together no man shall separate. We realize that our husbands are not our enemy. Therefore, we seal our marriages with your blood through the weapon of prayer. For the weapons of our warfare are not carnal but mighty through God to the pulling down of strongholds. We come against the enemy and bind every flirtatious spirit, adultery, pornography, selfishness, alcohol and drugs, anger, unforgiveness, and anything outside of the sanctity of marriage in Jesus name! God we ask that you direct our husbands to your word so their efforts will be honored by their commitment first to you and then to us.

We thank you for a new level of commitment in our marriage. We believe that you will perfect that which concerns us. Since you are God we place these and all things into your hands because you do all things well, in Jesus name, Amen!

Declaration: I declare by faith that (your husband's name) is fully committed to God and the covenant of marriage. He is considerate, tenderhearted, courteous, loving and kind. He has put on the Lord Jesus Christ and makes no provision for the flesh to fulfill its lusts. He is a blessed man who endures temptation because God is faithful to make a way of escape so that he is able to bare it. He is not broken down by the power of evil but raised up by the power of God.

Your role: "Pray without ceasing".
(1 Thessalonians 5:17) (KJV)
A wife of noble character: (Proverbs 31:10-31) (KJV)

"And unto the married I command, yet not I, but the Lord, Let not the wife depart from her husband".
(1 Corinthians 7:10) (KJV)

Stay encouraged and HOPE in God!

WEEK FOUR: COMMUNICATION

Let us pray,

I will bless the Lord at all times and his praise shall continually be in my mouth! Heavenly Father, once again we your daughters come boldly to your throne of grace. Before we ask you anything, we confess our sins and pray you will forgive us from all unrighteousness in the name of Jesus.

We ask your blessings upon our lips so that the words we speak to our husbands will be fruitful and pleasing to you. You said life and death are in the power of the tongue so teach us to speak words that build them up and not tare them down in Jesus name. We ask you to show us how to create an atmosphere that will make them feel comfortable to come to us and share the issues of their hearts. Teach us when to shut it down so we don't become nagging wives. Help us study to be quiet and give them our undivided attention. We want to be the kind of wives that keep peace in our marriage first through our submission to you and then to our husbands. You said out of the mouth, the heart speaks so we ask you to fill their hearts with your love so the words they speak will bring forth good things and not evil. We ask you to help our husbands relax and release tension that comes from the cares of this world. We invite your Holy Spirit to direct them to cast all of their cares upon you. We don't want them to be so stressed that they aren't able to engage in simple conversation with us. We realize that men and women communicate differently so help us to be patient with one another. We ask you to help us especially when our husbands don't respond when and how we feel they should. Teach us to respect the way they process information, to realize that they hear us, and to be patient until they respond. As you teach us, we pray that you will teach them to practice patience with us and help them understand our desire to express ourselves openly to them. We pray that you help us deal with issues when we don't agree so that we don't become disrespectful to one another. Help us see the warning signs in non-verbal communication that may speak silent frustration and show us how to deal with the root of it. We pray that you teach us how to affirm our husbands through a soft touch that says, I love you, I'm praying for you, I support you and everything is going to be alright!

Father we lift our concerns to you because you are our helper. We realize that only you can touch their heart and teach them how to express themselves so that our communication will remain open and effective. We thank you for the shifting that is taking place right now. We come against every evil spirit that attempts to hinder our communication. We speak death to anger, wrath, malice, blasphemy, disrespect, and filthy language. We shut the mouth of the enemy with our praise. We praise you for the good work you began in our marriage. We thank you for your Holy Spirit and for giving us what to say in every situation. We thank you for making us quick to hear and slow to speak. We praise you for seasoning our words with grace. We exalt your name, we brag on you Lord. Father you're so great you're in a class all by yourself, you're all inclusive. You're able to do anything but fail! You are the most-high God and no one else can ever take your place. We hollow your name, Hallelujah! Who is like our God? There is nobody like you! You are worthy to be praised! We declare that you are God enough to handle ALL things concerning us and we thank you in advance in Jesus name, amen!

Declaration: I declare by faith that (your husband's name) is a wise man. He loves the Lord therefore he loves, honors, and respects me in the way he speaks to me. He does not speak words that are corrupt, but words that are full of grace. He does not talk negatively or speak words that bring destruction. He speaks words that bring forth life, express the love, peace, and joy of the Lord!

Your role: Pray without ceasing".
(1 Thessalonians 5:17) (KJV)

A soft answer turneth away wrath: but grievous words stir up anger. Proverbs 15:1

Let the words of my mouth, and the meditation of my heart, be acceptable in thy sight, O LORD, my strength, and my redeemer. Psalm 19:14

Stay encouraged and HOPE in God!

WEEK FIVE: HEALTH-PROSPERITY

Let us pray,

It is a good thing to give thanks unto the Lord and to sing praises to your name O most high. Good morning Holy Spirit, we enter into your gates with thanksgiving and into your courts with praise. We declare that you are Jehovah God and there is no other like you. We come with repentant hearts asking you to cleanse us and forgive us from all unrighteousness in the name of Jesus.

We lift our husbands to you, thanking you for their life, health, and strength. We pray that you bless them to prosper and be in health even as their souls prosper. Remind them that their body is the temple of the Holy Spirit and give them a desire to care for it accordingly. Let no unclean thing dwell in them in Jesus name. Father we ask you to show us how to encourage them to take better care of themselves so that they may have life and that more abundantly. Give us words to speak that will minister hope to them in every situation. Teach us practical things we can do to help, like cooking healthier meals and bringing the proper foods into our homes instead of things that are not good for them. Father we know that as we do this we too must work to maintain a healthier lifestyle so we ask you to help us as we seek to do the right thing.

We pray for all who are dealing with any form of illness whether it be mentally, physically, emotionally or spiritually. We thank you for being a keeper and for what you have not allowed to happen. They are still here by the grace of God and for that we say, thank you! We know that sickness is not of you so we bind it all and every negative spirit that comes from it in the name of Jesus. We bind stress, anxiety, depression, suicide and anything that is against your will for their lives. We believe the report of the Lord that says you are able to do exceeding and abundantly above all we can ask or think. You are Jehovah Rapha, Lord God our healer! You are able to deliver them from all manner of sickness and disease. We plead the blood of Jesus and ask that you stretch your hand and let your healing power sweep through their entire body and restore their health completely in the name of Jesus. We ask that you usher in a spirit a peace that will rest upon them and keep them in the process. Look upon every prayer request, heal every disease and redeem their lives from destruction in Jesus name. You said that life and death are in the power of the tongue so we speak health, healing and long life over our husbands in Jesus name!

We pray that you anoint our husbands with the power to get wealth. Bless them in the work place and in their respective businesses. Give them new ideas and strategic plans that will cause them to prosper. We pray for the favor of God to rest upon them. Father we know the heart of the king is in your hand so we ask you to release a harvest of blessing upon them. We pray for those who are in need of employment. We know there is no thing too hard for you. We ask you to open the windows of heaven and pour them out a blessing they won't have room enough to receive. Bless them with a job that they will enjoy and one that will be more than enough to cover the financial needs of our family. We speak jobs and better jobs, promotions, bonuses, settlements and increase in every area of their life. We pray that you give them balance and help them to keep our family their number one priority. Help them pull away from work mode and not deprive their family of the time they need together. Father as you bless them; give them a heart to give back, first to you in paying their tithes and offering. Show them that you can bless the 90% that remains far better than they can hold onto the 100% in disobedience to your word. As they freely give to you, give them a heart to reach out and help others who may be in need. We speak your word over our husbands and declare that as they give it shall be given unto them, good measure, pressed down, shaken together, and running over, shall men give into their bosom.

Father as you prosper them financially, we pray that their souls would prosper. We pray for an increase in their knowledge of who you are. Increase their love for you. Increase their desire to obey you. Increase their witness of who you are. Give them a hunger and thirst after you! Remind them to seek first your kingdom and your righteousness in all that they do and all other things will be added unto them. As you do these things for them, we pray that you get all the glory, honor and praise in Jesus name, Amen!

Declaration: I declare by faith, that by your stripes, (your husband's name) is healed in the name of Jesus! He has peace in his heart, mind, body and spirit and he shall live to declare the works of the Lord. There is no lack in (your husband's name) life, his cup is full and overflowing with the blessing of the Lord that maketh rich and adds no sorrow.

Your role: "Pray without ceasing".
(1 Thessalonians 5:17) (KJV)

"Don't worry about anything; instead, pray about everything. Tell God what you need, and thank him for all he has done". (Philippians 4:6) (NLT)

Stay encouraged and HOPE in God!

WEEK SIX: RELATIONSHIPS

Let us pray,

Oh give thanks unto the Lord, for He is good! For his mercy endures forever. Father in the name of Jesus we praise you for your grace and mercy. Because of you we have the testimony that we are still here united as one with our spouse in Holy matrimony. We come touching and agreeing that there is no friend like you. We confess our sins and ask you to forgive us for anything we have done against your will. Make and mold us into the women of God you created us to be. We ask that you continue to teach us how to be a godly wife to our husband. We surrender our will and invite you to have your way in our lives in Jesus name.

Father we thank you for another opportunity to lift our husbands to you. We ask that you continue to nurture and develop them into the men of God you created them to be. Teach them how to nourish and cultivate their relationship with you. Remind them that because they have been reconciled through the blood of Jesus, there is no need to feel intimidated when they fall short of your glory. Remind them to go boldly to your throne of grace where they can obtain mercy and compassion. Give them a heart that is quick to repent with a desire for a right relationship with you. We ask that you pour out your spirit upon them and give them a desire to love you so they can fully love us in ways that bring glory to your name. We ask you to help us love them in the same way. Show us how to be a true friend so they will have a desire to spend time with us, share with us, and love us with the love of God. Teach us to forgive and show us how to rebuild those areas in our relationship that have been damaged. We pray for an increase of love and understanding that will cause us to be more considerate of one another. Make us sensitive to their need for affirmation, affection and all those things that encourage them and make them feel loved and appreciated. We pray that you sensitize them in the same way as it relates to our needs in the marriage. We bind the spirit of selfishness, division, and anything that will hinder us from growing closer together as one flesh. We pray that you will knit our hearts together with cords of love that cannot be separated. We plead the blood of Jesus and cancel the plan of the enemy to destroy us through relationships outside of our marriage. We declare that what you have joined together, no man shall separate in Jesus name. We ask that you give us mutual friendships with other couples so we can bond through fellowship as we seek to grow and mature in our marriage. We pray for love, respect, honor, and trust in Jesus name!

We lift up their relationships with family members and friends. Give them a desire to have relationship with their children, parents and siblings. We pray that you will move on their hearts and show them the importance of bonding with their children. Help them to see the level of influence and the power you have given them to speak life into their children. We pray that they will honor their parents so that they may have long life upon the earth. Increase the level of relationship they share with their siblings as you use them as an example of your goodness and grace. We pray that they will display the fruit of the spirit in their lives by the way they love and forgive. We speak liberty in Christ Jesus over their minds and pray that they will not hold on to issues of the past. We bind confusion, disagreements, and unforgiveness. We ask you to mend all family relationships especially those that have damaged their self-esteem through any form of abuse and neglect.

You said that iron sharpens iron so we ask you to join them together with Christian brothers who will serve as mentors and the kind of friends that will build them up and hold them accountable to your standard. Surround them with men of God who have made up their mind to touch not, taste not, nor handle the unclean things of this world. Show them how to gain good friendships by first showing themselves friendly. Teach them not to walk out when things don't go their way. Remind them of your word that says a friend loves at all times. We pray for discernment so they will recognize the difference between a true friend and those who are seeking after their own gain. Father we thank you in advance for a new level of love and appreciation in the area of relationships. We praise you and give you the glory for the great things you have done in Jesus name, Amen!

Declaration: I declare by faith that (your husband's name) is a friend of God. His relationship with the Lord is his number one priority. He loves me with the love of God and honors the vows we have made to one another. We are best friends! I declare that (your husband's name) is free from the bondage of unforgiveness. His relationships with family members and friends are healthy, and pleasing in the sight of God.

Your role: "Pray without ceasing".
(1 Thessalonians 5:17) (KJV)

"Who can find a virtuous and capable wife? She is more precious than rubies. Her husband can trust her, and she will greatly enrich his life. She brings him good, not harm, all the days of her life".
(Proverbs 31:10-12) (NLT)

"Give all your worries and cares to God, for he cares about you". (1 Peter 5:7) (NLT)

Stay encouraged and HOPE in God!

"My Condition

is not

My Conclusion!"

~Rev. Dr. Winston C. Ridley, Jr.

"Thou shalt also decree a thing, and it shall be established unto thee: and the light shall shine upon thy ways." Job 22:28

PRAYER AND FASTING FOR OUR CHILDREN

Children are the heritage of the Lord, they are a gift from God and should be loved, nurtured, cherished and raised in the admonition of the Lord. We decree that because our God is faithful, he will establish our children and keep them from the evil one. As you pray and fast, insert the name of your child(ren) in the declaration statements.

Week 1   Spiritual Growth
Week 2   Plead the Blood
Week 3   Health
Week 4   Relationships
Week 5   Protection
Week 6   Future
Week 7   Thanksgiving

WEEK ONE: SPIRITUAL GROWTH

Let us pray,

Father in the name of Jesus, we bless and adore your Holy name. We exalt you for who you are. You are the Great I am! You are Master, Savior, Lord, and King. We enter into your gates with thanksgiving and into your courts with praise. Great and Mighty are you Lord! Father as we approach your throne on behalf of our children, we confess our sins and ask your forgiveness in the name of Jesus. Search our hearts and remove anything that is not pleasing in your sight.

We come before as mothers, aunties, godmothers, grandmothers, foster moms, and moms to be on this first week of prayer and fasting. Your word says if we agree on earth concerning anything that we ask, it will be done for us by our Father in heaven. We touch and agree in the area of Spiritual Growth for our children. Before we lift them to you we ask for wisdom and guidance for every season of their lives. Help us live the life of Christ before them and not become mere dictators living contrary to your word. Strengthen our husbands as you raise them up to have spiritual influence in the lives of our children. Remind us of the power in prayer as we anoint and pray with and for them. Your word says if we train our children in the way they should go, when they are old they will not depart from it. Send your Holy Spirit to increase in the lives of our children as we seek to nurture and bring them up in the word of God. Show us how to teach them to love, honor and respect the things of God. Remind us of examples in your word that can be applied to their lives both young and old in the name of Jesus. Give them a hunger and thirst to continue in the path of righteousness. Remind us that our children are human and that sometimes they will make decisions that will disappoint. Show us how to deal with it and continue to love and forgive them as you do for us. Give them a WWJD moment so the next time their decision will line up with your will and not their want, in the name of Jesus! As they go through life, let us not waiver in our faith but keep prayer on our lips. Remind us of the good work you began in them and that you have the power to finish what you started! According to your word, we have the power to decree a thing and it shall be established. We call them saved, sanctified and filled with the Holy Ghost. They acknowledge you as Lord and Savior. They know, understand and live by the word of God. We plead the blood of Jesus over their hearts and minds and declare them to be the righteousness of God! The word of God shall speak in their lives and not return unto you void. They shall bear fruit that brings glory and honor to your name. We speak life to those who have strayed from your word because you are not slack concerning your promises. We thank you for being patient and giving them space and time to change. We declare that our children shall love the Lord thy God, they shall have no other gods before you, and they SHALL serve you and you alone, in the name of Jesus! We speak death to every plot designed to hinder their spiritual growth and separate them from you. We come against the rulers of darkness of this world and spiritual wickedness in high places in the name of Jesus! We plead the blood as we speak to the enemy and render him powerless in the name of Jesus! We call him the father of lies and declare that NO weapon formed against our children will prosper. Father we thank you in advance for increase in their spiritual growth. We praise you for every mighty man of valour and virtuous woman covered in this prayer. We rest in the assurance that ALL things are working together for their good in Jesus name, Amen!

Declaration: I declare by faith that, _____ is growing spiritually, he/she is not conformed to the things of this world but being transformed into a new person by the way he/she thinks. _____ is learning to know God's will, which is good and pleasing and perfect in the name of Jesus!

Stay encouraged and HOPE in God!

WEEK TWO: PLEAD THE BLOOD

Praise the Lord Women of God,

This week we are pleading the blood of Jesus over our children. I know it might look like the enemy is winning in your situation but you must remember that the Blood will NEVER lose its power! If you're in need of a miracle I have good news for you, the blood reaches to the highest mountain and flows to the lowest valley so it doesn't matter what season of life your child or children are going through, the blood will prevail through the power of prayer! Come on women of God this is warfare, we already have the victory so don't you dare allow the enemy to stop you from praying and fasting for your children. He's a liar and a defeated foe! Now is the time for us to let the devil know that we are not under a curse, the buck stops with us, were going to start decreeing some generational blessings over our kids right now, in the name of Jesus!

Stay encouraged and HOPE in God!

WEEK THREE: HEALTH

Let us pray,

Father in the name of Jesus, we thank you for
another opportunity to bless and praise your Holy
name. You said in all things to give you thanks so
we come collectively thanking you for the gift of
our children. Because we know it is your desire
that they prosper and be in health, we're standing in
the gap praying for their mental, emotional,
physical and spiritual health. Before we ask you
anything we repent of all sin and unrighteousness
and pray you will forgive us in the name of Jesus.
Thank you for being a loving God that we can come
to just as we are and find you to be the same
yesterday, today and forever more.

Father we pray that you would make us good
examples to our children in the way we take care of
ourselves. Let them see us feast on your word to
feed our minds on thoughts that line up with your
word and not this world. Make us the kind of
parents that are willing to communicate our feelings
with our children as well as listen to them so that
we do not become a family bound by emotional
stress or hurt. Help us be good stewards over our
bodies making appointments for regular check-ups
for ourselves as well as our children. We ask that
you help us to be consistent in our walk with you,
our prayer life as well as the example we set before
them spiritually in the name of Jesus. Father we

recognize that there may be wives connected to this prayer who have a desire to bare children but have not been blessed to do so. We pray that you will touch both husband and wife healing their bodies from anything that stands in the way of them being fruitful and adding to their family. We pray that you will do so that they will have a legacy to raise in the fear and admonition of your Holy name. We know there is nothing too hard for you so we are touching and agreeing that as they walk up right before you, you will grant them the desires of their heart. While they stand believing you for this blessing, bless them for the love they continue to extend to another child in the name of Jesus!

Father we lift the health of our children before you. We know sickness does not come from you so we bind every manner of sickness and disease that has come to kill, steal and destroy. Send your Holy Spirit to rest upon their minds so that they may have perfect peace in the name of Jesus. We come against mental illness, confusion and every mental disorder declaring that they have a sound mind in the name of Jesus. We bind every evil spirit that comes to torture them mentally causing them to have thoughts of hatred and suicide in the name of Jesus. We plead the blood and speak your word that declares they shall have life and that more abundantly. We pray for their emotional health as we thank you for healing them from medical disorders, the affects that have come from broken relationships, low self-esteem and anything that has caused them to be emotionally unstable. We plead the blood of Jesus and invite your Holy Spirit to pour out a double portion of your love that will regulate and stabilize them emotionally. We know you to be a heart fixer so we ask you to fix it Jesus as only you can. We come against the spirit of the enemy that would give them a desire to mark up and pierce their bodies. We speak death to it and declare their body to be the temple of the Holy Spirit, in the name of Jesus. We demand all pain and suffering to flee from them in the name of Jesus. Your word says that the prayer prayed in faith will heal the sick. Father we believe you to be Jehovah Rapha, the healer of all diseases, therefore, we declare there will be no disease, infection or anything that will dwell in them. We ask you to heal their bodies and bring comfort to them as we encourage them to trust you through the healing process.

Teach them to trust you at all times, even those who have been hurt in the church. We pray that you will mend the broken places in their hearts and not allow the enemy to use situations or people to separate them from you. Give them a personal relationship with you that no matter what happens they will choose to pick up their cross and follow you in the name of Jesus. If they have strayed from you, we pray that you will restore them into a right relationship that will give them a deeper hunger and thirst for your righteousness. We thank you for being our God, for inclining your ear to this prayer, and for healing them completely in the name of Jesus!

Declaration: I decree the word of God over _____ life. For he was wounded for _____transgressions, he was bruised for _____ iniquities; the chastisement of _____ peace was upon him and with his stripes _____ is healed mentally, emotionally, physically and spiritually in the name of Jesus!

Stay encouraged and HOPE in God!

WEEK FOUR: RELATIONSHIPS

Let us pray,

Father in the name of Jesus we give thanks unto
your name because you are the Most High God and
you are worthy of all praise! We pray for
forgiveness of all sin in the name of Jesus.

We come this day with singing in our hearts as we
pray for our children. What a friend we have in
Jesus, all our sins and grieves to bare. What a
privilege it is to carry everything to God in prayer!
We come casting our cares upon you because we
know that you care for us. Your word says you love
them that love you. Thank you for loving us and for
being a friend like none other. You have been
everything a true friend could be and so much more.
You remained a friend when we turned our backs
on you. You even forgave us and helped us through
the faults and failures we brought upon ourselves.
As we pray for the relationships of our children, we
ask you to be the same kind of a friend to them that
you have been to us. Father we ask you to help us
examine ourselves and the relationships we share
with our children. Give us wisdom to correct those
areas where we need to be better parents. Show us
how to deal with the affects that come from their
relationships with others. Help us model your
character in our families that will set the standard of
what our children would consider a true friend. Just
as you are, make us loving, kind, and faithful to

them as they seek friendships in play mates, best friends and mates. We plead the blood and pray that their relationship with you will be the first priority in their lives. We pray that they will be attracted to people who know you and love you! Help them choose those kinds of friends that make godly choices as we have trained them to do so. Let them recognize evil and flee from those things they know are not pleasing in your sight. We plead the blood over their hearts and minds asking you to make them the salt in the earth and not join with ungodly people who influence them to lower their standards in any way in the name of Jesus. We come against unhealthy relationships that cause our children to rebel, sinning against you and us. We plead the blood over disrespectful attitudes and behaviors that come from negative influences, especially those they consider a friend. We pray for relationships that are formed in school, on their jobs, and amongst their peers. We know that you are able to keep them from falling and that in every moment of temptation you will make a way of escape so make them wise in their choices and decisions choosing good and not evil.

We pray for a spirit of oneness for those who are married. Give them a determination to endure the good and bad as you mold them together as one. We bind the spirit of divorce and declare it will not be named among our children. Make us the example of Holy Matrimony as they walk through the different seasons together. Let them see us love and forgive in the name of Jesus. We bind the spirit of the enemy and every trick he uses in the attempt to kill, steal and destroy our children. We plead the blood and declare that our children belong to you. We pray for their friends, if they are not saved, let the God in our children influence them towards a desire to have a relationship with you. Thank you for connecting our children with people whose lives represent and honor you in the name of Jesus, Amen!

Declaration: I declare that
_____ is covered by the blood of Jesus and he/she is more than a conqueror! Because the prayers of the righteous are availing much, _____ is connected to Godly/wholesome relationships that encourage him/her to fulfill God's purpose in his/her life.

Stay encouraged and HOPE in God!

WEEK FIVE: PROTECTION

Let us pray,

Father in the name of Jesus, we come before you touching and agreeing that you are a Great and Mighty God! There is no one like you! You are King of kings and Lord of lords and we love you for who you are! We ask you to give us clean hands and pure hearts so that nothing will hinder our prayer.

We come before you declaring your word over our children as it relates to their Protection. Thank you for being omnipresent, because you are everywhere at the same time we can rest in the fact that you are watching over them. Your word says you never slumber nor sleep so we don't have to worry, we can pray and rest in you. We confess now for the times when we placed situations into your hands concerning our children and then took it back out of anxiety and tried to work it out ourselves. Forgive us Lord and receive our prayer on this day as we pray and fast according to your word. Thank you for being a safe haven for our children, a shelter in the time of storm, a refuge and strong tower against the hand of the enemy. We give you praise for protecting them from all hurt harm and danger. Thank you for watching over our little babies, our adolescence, teens and adult sons and daughters. We recognize that it has been you who canceled the enemy's plans to destroy them. You have kept them from kidnappers, rapist, abusers, murderers, and robbers. We thank you and declare that our children are protected by your blood. They will not be manipulated into negative relationships because of low self-esteem or trapped into evil doing. We plead the blood over every babysitter, teacher, and employer. We come against accidents and incidents related to transportation. The blood over school buses, cars, trains, airplanes, and the vehicles our children operate themselves. The blood over every place their feet trod, we declare they are safe in the arms of Jesus! We plead the blood of Jesus over their minds as your word says there is a way that seems right to man but that road leads to destruction. We pray that you protect them against the spirit of confusion, foolish thinking and hasty decision making in the name of Jesus! We declare that they will trust in you with all their heart and lean not unto their own understanding knowing that you will direct their path. We bind the spirit of fear and doubt and declare your word that you will never leave nor forsake them but you will be with our children, always. We speak peace to their thoughts and declare they have sound minds in the name of Jesus! Father we trust that you have all things in and under control. We declare that the enemy is under our feet therefore we render him powerless in the name of Jesus! Thank you Lord for loving our children so much that you protect them even when they neglect you. You are just that kind of God who changes not!

We stand in the gap for our children and bless you for remaining faithful at all times and in all things. Great is thy faithfulness Lord unto us! We acknowledge your hand upon their lives and thank you for inclining your ear to our prayers on their behalf in Jesus name, Amen!

Declaration: I declare that He shall give his angels charge over _____, to keep him/her in all thy ways. Psalm 91:11

I declare that _____ will not be afraid of the enemy, for the LORD my God himself will fight for him/her. Deut 3:22 NIV

I declare that _____ will be strong and courageous, Lord, for your word says, "Do not be afraid or terrified because of them, for the LORD your God goes with you; He will never leave you nor forsake you." Deut 31:6 NIV

I declare that when _____ passes through the waters, you will be with him/her; and when he/she passes through the rivers, they will not sweep over _____. When _____ walks through the fire, he/she will not be burned; the flames will not set me ablaze. (Isaiah 43:2 NIV)

I declare that the LORD shall fight for _____, and he/she shall hold his/her peace. I declare that no weapon formed against _____ shall prosper, and every tongue which rises against him/her in judgment he/she shall condemn. This is the heritage of the servants of the LORD, and their righteousness is from me, says the LORD. Isaiah 54:17

But let all (our children) take refuge in you and be glad; let them ever sing for joy. Spread your PROTECTION over them that those who love your name may rejoice in you. Psalm 5:11

My son /daughter, forget not my law, but let thine heart keep my commandments; For length of days, and long life, and peace, shall they add to thee. Let not mercy and truth forsake thee; bind them about thy neck write them upon the table of thine heart. So shalt thou find favour and good understanding in the sight of God and man. Trust in the Lord with all thine heart; and lean not unto thine own understanding. In all thy ways acknowledge him, and he shall direct thy paths. Proverbs 1:1-6

Stay encouraged and HOPE in God!

WEEK SIX: FUTURE

Let us pray,

Father in the name of Jesus, we praise you for another day. We declare you to be a Holy God. We exalt your name and declare there is no one like you. You're in a class all by yourself. You're all inclusive, there is no lack in you. You are all powerful, you're in control of everything. We praise you for who you are!   Before we ask anything we pray that you will forgive us of all sin so there will be nothing to hinder our prayer this day.

We come before you lifting the future of our children to you. Father we pray that you will lead and guide them into all truth. We ask you to endow them with wisdom and discernment so that as they may choices along the journey of life they will be righteous and those that line up with your will. We thank you for allowing us to belong to you. We know that with you there is nothing that shall be impossible for our children. We pray that they will see you as the limitless God who has no boundaries. Help them to see that because of you they can dream BIG, they can aim HIGH and they can secure a future that will be prosperous first by acknowledging you in all of their ways so they will have eternal life. Let them not be intimated but reach beyond their imagination and allow the Holy Spirit to direct their paths even when the process

62

seems overwhelming. Remind them that you are the God who sits high yet looks low. You are Alpha and Omega, you sit at the beginning and the end of everything. We pray that our children will be obedient as you have commanded in your word so that they may have long life to enjoy the manifold blessings you will bestow upon them. Give them a mind to obey your commands and recognize that you are all knowing and that they need you in all things. When our children make even the smallest choices we pray that they will seek to please you in their decisions. Your word says you love those who love you and when they seek you they will find you. We thank you for being a present help and pray that they will seek you at the beginning of all they do and not just when trouble comes. When they have made the wrong choice we pray that you will have mercy upon them and redirect their desires to align with your will and not their wants. We pray your word over them now and declare that as they seek you first and your righteousness, all other things will be added unto them. We pray that they will be anxious for nothing, but by pray and supplication and with thanksgiving, they will make their request known unto you. We pray your word that when our children call upon you, you will incline your ear to hear their prayers. When they are not sure of which way to turn they will stand still and see your salvation, they will wait upon you for wisdom and direction.

We touch and agree with the dreams and visions that are brewing in their hearts and minds right now. We declare that they shall be all that you created them to be. We praise you for giving us a mind to pray for the future of all of our children. Help us to stir up the gifts you have placed in them, especially at an early age, as well as encourage those who are at a crossroad in life. We pray for wisdom on how to reach and encourage our adult children who have settled and have not yet become productive. We bind generational curses and all those things that hinder them from securing a prosperous future. We speak life to their dreams and visions and declare that they shall live and not die and have life even more abundantly in Jesus name, Amen!

Declaration: For I know the thoughts that I think toward _____, saith the LORD, thoughts of peace, and not of evil, to give _____ an expected end. I declare that _____ is strong and courageous. He/she is neither terrified nor discouraged, for the Lord thy God is with him/her. I declare that _____ will trust in the Lord with all his/her heart and lean not to his/her own understanding. _____ shall acknowledge the Lord in all of his/her ways and He will make _____'s path straight. I declare that _____ is above only and not beneath, the head and not the tail. I declare that God's purpose for _____ shall prevail!

Stay encouraged and HOPE in God!

WEEK SEVEN: THANKSGIVING

Let us pray,

Father in the name of Jesus, great is thy faithfulness unto us! We come before your throne of grace to thank you for new mercies on this day. We sing praises unto your name because you are the Most High God. How Great thou art! Thank you for life, health and strength! We exalt your name because you are our God and there is no one like you! We give you praise and honor because you are worthy to be praised! From the rising of the sun until the going down of the same, we will bless your Holy name. Father as we bow before you to say thank you, we first ask you to wash and cleanse of everything that is not like you. Transform our minds even while we're praying so that our thoughts will be conformed to your will and your way.

Father we come today to say thank you for the privilege you have given us to stand in the gap for our children as we have prayed and fasted these past seven weeks. Thank you for giving us power over the enemy. We know the number seven denotes the completion of a thing. We have sealed our children with prayer as we have decreed your word over their lives. We have spoken death to everything that is not like you and life to everything that lines up with your word. We have reminded the enemy that he is a defeated foe and everything he planned is Over, Dead, Finished and Powerless in their lives in Jesus name! Today we just want to say thank you for giving us a mind to touch and agree and most importantly to lift them before you. Our words seem so inadequate to describe our gratefulness to you so we simply say, thank you Lord!

Thank you Lord for being our hiding place and shield our HOPE is in your word and not what we see with our natural eyes. As we touch and agree, we speak your word because we know that you are careful to watch over it so that it may be performed in the lives of our children. We thank you that our children are growing spiritually in you because with you there is unfailing love and an overflowing supply of salvation. Thank you Father for cleansing them and making them whole in the name of Jesus! We give you praise for the blood of Jesus that covers our children. Because of you are in control of their lives, no weapon formed against them will prosper. Thank you for the road blocks you have set up so they won't go too far to the left or to the right. When the enemy rushes in like a flood we can rest assure that the blood of Jesus will protect our children, the blood will shield, and the blood will deliver from everything that is not like you, in Jesus name! We agree with your word that our children will prosper and be in health even as their soul prospers. We declare healing in their bodies by the stripes you bore on Calvary. We declare that our children have cheerful hearts, your words says, it is doing them good just like medicine. Thank you for being a healer of their mind, body and spirit! Thank you for being a friend to our children, with you they will never be alone because you promised never to leave nor forsake them. Thank you Father for how you are renewing our relationship with them. We praise you that nothing will be able to separate our love, communication and respect towards one another. Thank you for the wholesome friendships you are placing in their lives, you are giving them friends that love and acknowledge you as Lord. We praise you for helping our children to keep themselves pure so that they can be used for your purpose. We declare that their lives are clean and they will be ready to be used by you for every good work in Jesus name! Father we thank you for being their protection and for dispatching angels to watch over them. We declare your blood covering that no hurt, harm or danger will come nye their dwelling. They are safe in your arms at the daycare, in school, on their jobs, in their homes and every place their feet trod in Jesus name! Thank you for the good thoughts you have towards our children. We declare their future is bright and that nothing shall be impossible with you!

Father we thank you for your word that says when we call upon you, you will incline your ear to hear our prayers. We pray that you continue to bless them, draw them nye unto you, lead them in your path of righteousness, talk with them and teach them your will. We believe you are able to do exceeding and abundantly above all we can ask or think. We thank you for what you have done, what you are doing for what our eyes hath not seen, our ears hath not heard and for the things that has not entered into our hearts concerning your plans for our children. We love and bless you in Jesus name, Amen!

Declaration: I declare that
_____ loves the Lord with all his/her heart. _____is obedient/respectful to his/her parents therefore he/she shall have long life upon the earth!
I declare that _____has increased in wisdom and stature and in favor with God and man.
I declare that _____ is the righteousness of God! _____ is a Mighty Man of Valour! _____ is a Virtuous Woman!
I declare that _____ has been set apart for God's purpose and glory! The Lord will prevail in _____'s life in Jesus name!

Stay encouraged and HOPE in God!

"I cannot afford to believe anything other than what I believe God to do!"

~Co-Pastor Susie C. Owens

"Blessed is she that believed that there shall be a performance of those things spoken to her by the Lord." Luke 1:45

HANNAH'S HOPE

Praise the Lord Women of God!

This is the day the Lord has made, let us rejoice and be glad in it! Several years ago I began to partner in prayer with a wife believing that the Lord would bless her with a child. The Lord did just that, her testimony is posted on the website at: www.touchandagreeministries.org.

We are believing the Lord to extend grace on your behalf as we touch and agree (Matt. 18:19).

EQUIPPED FOR THE PROMISE

Let us pray,

Father in the matchless name of Jesus, we thank you for the opportunity to come boldly before your throne of grace. We praise you for being God Almighty! You are the only true, wise and living God and besides you there is no other! We come to agree with your word believing that some things come only by prayer and fasting. We first ask your forgiveness of all unrighteousness in Jesus name!

We come as Hannah's and Prayer Warriors speaking the truth of your word that says if we abide in you and your word in us we could ask anything and you will do it! Since we have your word in us we ask you to open the womb of every Hannah petitioning you for a child. We bind all distractions from every Hannah connected to this prayer and pray that you sensitize our spiritual ears so that we hear your voice only. We stand strong in your power and your might as we use our spiritual weapons to cancel and destroy everything that is contrary to your will and speak life to what we believe. We put on the Whole Armour of God so that there will be no room for the spirit of doubt, anxiety, fear, failure or disbelief in Jesus name! We know you to be the omnipotent God, the giver of life with all power to bring it to pass. We rebuke plans of the enemy and speak the truth of your word to every doctor's report, every negative test and hindrance and decree that Nothing shall be impossible with you! Because of your righteousness we decree and declare that we are protected from all hurt harm and danger. We rebuke barrenness, miscarriages and unhealthy pregnancies, and call forth new life in Jesus name! We rebuke depression, stress, confusion, anger, disappointment and decree an atmosphere of your perfect peace. We hold fast to our faith knowing that it is your desire that we be fruitful and multiply. We know and believe that you can do anything but fail! We cover our minds with the helmet of salvation to guard our minds against every thought that is not of you. We decree that we have the mind of Christ, our thoughts are above only and not beneath! Our attitudes are healthy, positive and whole. We think on things that are lovely, just and of a good report.

Since you are the God of all HOPE we stand on your word that says you are able to do exceeding abundantly above all we can ask or think. For every tear we decree beauty for ashes, for the spirit of heaviness we decree a garment of praise, for the spirit of hopelessness we decree a great expectation of new life! We Believe the Report of the Lord in the name of Jesus, Amen!

Stay encouraged and HOPE in God!

PERSISTENT PRAYER

Let us pray,

I will lift up mine eyes unto the hills from whence cometh my help, my help comes from the Lord which made heaven and earth. Father in the name of Jesus, we need you every hour. We come boldly before your throne standing in the need of prayer. We ask for your forgiveness of all sin and unrighteousness. Cleanse us from everything that goes against you. Make and mold us after your own will. Create in us a clean heart and renew within us a right spirit. We come confessing what you already know, that is we cannot make it without you. It is in you that we live, move and have our being. It is in you that our very faith exists. We recognize that without faith it is impossible to please you. Father, we want to please you in all that we think, say and do. We want to honor your name and represent you in every area of our lives. We come asking for mercy this day. We want to be persistent in our prayers; we want to make our request known to you yet again because you are a consistent God. You are faithful in all of your ways. We believe you hear us when we pray and that you will heed to our cry. We cry out to you not in sadness of heart or hopelessness but we cry out to you as our daddy, our father and our all-powerful God! We're not looking to the left or the right. We're seeking your face. We're setting our petition before you because we know you are well able to bring it to pass. Our spirits are leaping with joy because we have not come alone but we've come with like-minded women of God who know who you are and believe you like we do. You said if any two of us touch and agree you would do it for us. We believe to hear testimony upon testimony of how you have blessed Hannah to conceive. Not only so but we believe that when they come forth your anointing will be upon their lives and all will know that they have been set apart for your glory. You said if we believe in our hearts without doubt or fear, we would have what we say. We coming with a united voice this day to say we believe you Lord! We wait patiently yet expectantly for you to show up and show out! You said if there are any mountains in our way we could speak to them and cause them to be removed. We speak to sickness, marital conflict, doubt, fear, stress and every area that would hinder these pregnancies from coming forth. We plead the blood of Jesus and command them to flee in Jesus name.

We call forth total healing, the peace of God and believe that we receive what we ask of you. We decree it to be so! We thank you for hearing and answering our prayer, in Jesus name, amen!

Stay encouraged and HOPE in God!

PURSUE PEACE

Let us pray,

Father in the name of Jesus we praise you for the privilege of prayer and the opportunity to give honor to your name. We exalt you and declare that you are great and greatly to be praised! From the rising of the sun until the going down of the same you alone are worthy! We come with humble hearts asking your forgiveness for anything that might hinder this prayer. We want to be right before you so purge and cleanse us from all unrighteousness in the name of Jesus.

We come with joyful hearts to bless you for who you are. You are Jehovah Shalom, the God peace! You are our peacemaker in the time of storms. You're our daddy the one we can call on to calm every wind and wave. Thank you for giving us the assurance that we can find rest in you. When our hearts are overwhelmed we can run to you, our solid rock! We come this day to remind ourselves that we have peace with you! We don't come anxious about our petition, we come in a spirit of peace, prayer and thanksgiving. We're making our request known unto you and placing it in your most capable hands. Since you own time we wait patiently on you to act because you know what's best for us and our times are in your hands. When the enemy rushes in like a flood we can stand firm in your peace that surpasses all understanding. We can declare that you are an on time God, you're never late our steps are ordered by you! Thank for being a man of war that fights every battle we face in this life. Nothing comes as a surprise to you nor will anything ever be too hard for you! We know that everything we go through is working for our good and will not cancel your promise to us. You said NO weapon formed against us will prosper! Therefore we know no defeat, only Victory in Christ Jesus. We rebuke every trick and plan of the enemy that comes to disturb the peace in our minds, our marriage and our bodies. We command every disturbance in our lives to cease to exist in Jesus name! We plead the blood over our husbands and decree that everything sent to distract and destroy them is canceled in Jesus name! We send a message back to hell that it will NOT work! We decree a spirit of oneness between us so that our communion will be sweet. We decree that our relationship is sweet, our communication is sweet, and our companionship is sweet. Everything connected to our promise is a done deal! Where we have been weak we decree your everlasting strength in Jesus name! Your word says you will give strength to us and bless us with peace.

Since you are in complete control we make up our minds to rejoice at all times even when we have to wait a little longer, we will be patient in times of trouble and vow to be consistent like Hannah in our petition to you. We know that we cannot ask you too often because your word says pray without ceasing! In fact Hannah made her request known unto you daily. Father, we do the same not just today or this week. We don't just ask but we believe! Because we have your peace we can wait on you and trust your word that says you are good to those who wait. We stand on your promise to prosper us and bring us to an expected end! We thank you for your peace in Jesus name, amen!

Stay encouraged and HOPE in God!

ADVANCE PRAISE

Let us pray,

Father in the name of Jesus we come before you with thanksgiving and praise! Thank you for the opportunity to touch and agree with your word concerning our promise. We believe you Lord! We know you to be a promise keeper. We put on a garment of praise and decree that nothing shall be able to steal our joy! You are our God and we will praise you! There is no one like you! Hallelujah to the Lamb of God. Great and mighty is your name. If we had ten thousand tongues we could not praise you enough. If we praised you all day long for the rest of our lives we would still owe you praise. From the rising of the sun until the going down of the same you are worthy to be praised! You have turned our mourning into dancing! You have given us HOPE and filled us with gladness! You have increased our faith! Blessed be your Holy name. We bless you for past, present and future blessings. We honor you for your mighty works and declare that they are marvelous in our eyesight! We shout for joy for the favor that comes from your righteousness. Hosanna in the highest, blessed be the name of the Lord! We're not waiting until we receive the promise we're shouting now with a voice of triumph! We decree Victory in the name of Jesus, amen!

Now make it personal by adding your praise......

Stay encouraged and HOPE in God!

SCRIPTURE MEDITATION

"Elkanah knew Hannah his wife; and the LORD remembered her. Wherefore it came to pass, when the time was come about after Hannah had conceived, that she bare a son, and called his name Samuel, saying, Because I have asked him of the LORD." 1 Samuel 1:19b-20

"Through faith also Sara herself received strength to conceive seed, and was delivered of a child when she was past age, because she judged him faithful who had promised." Hebrews 11:11

Declare it: "And God remembered (your name) , and God hearkened to her, and opened her womb." Genesis 30:22

"For I will restore health unto thee, and I will heal thee of thy wounds, saith the LORD;" Jeremiah 30:17a

Declare it: I am healed of all sickness and diseases! "If ye abide in me, and my words abide in you, ye shall ask what ye will, and it shall be done unto you." John 15:7

Declare it: My hope is in the word of God therefore, what I have asked of the Lord will be done unto me!

"Therefore I say unto you, what things so ever ye desire, when ye pray, believe that ye receive them, and ye shall have them." Mark 11:24

Declare it: My tongue is the pen of a ready writer, I will conceive and bring forth a healthy child (children).

"Let us hold fast the profession of our faith without wavering; (for he is faithful that promised)" Hebrews 10:23

Declare it: I believe God!

Stay encouraged and HOPE in God!

"Rejoice in our confident HOPE. Be patient in trouble, and keep on praying."

Romans 12:12 (NLT)

Women of God, thank you for joining me in prayer and fasting for the family.

"If you can believe God for anything, you can believe Him for everything."

~Lisa C. Turner

"Now faith is the substance of things hoped for, the evidence of things not seen. [6] But without faith it is impossible to please him: for he that cometh to God must believe that he is, and that he is a rewarder of them that diligently seek him." Hebrews 11:1, 6

www.ingramcontent.com/pod-product-compliance
Lightning Source LLC
Chambersburg PA
CBHW060418050426
42449CB00009B/2023